PLUCKING CANTALOUPE

PLUCKING CANTALOUPE

KIARA MARIE

Copyright © 2021 by Kiara Marie.

All rights reserved. No part of this book may be used or reproduced in any manner whatsoever without the express written permission of the publisher except for the use of brief quotations in a book review.

Printed in the United States of America

ISBN: 978-1-7358701-2-0 (paperback)

   978-1-7358701-3-7 (ebook)

First printing, 2021

JayMedia Publishing

Laurel, MD 20708

www.publishing.jaymediagroup.net

Father above in the name of love,

I thank you for your blessings, sending peace to that which was, love for that which is, and excitement for that which is to be.

Amen

CONTENTS

I KNOW PT 1 1
BLACK WOMAN 3
CANVAS 5
HUH 7
BETTER DAYS 9
SPARROWS 11
JESUS IS COMING 13
PURPLE-BAG SKITTLES 17
CRAZY COASTER 19
NOT ANOTHER BROKEN-HEARTED BLACK WOMAN 21
STATUTE OF LIMITATIONS 25
BLOODY SHIT 27
ON THE GYNECOLOGIST OFFICE 29
HALLELUJAH 31
COKE WHITE & RAPUNZEL 33
BEAUTIFUL TODAY 37
ICE WATER 39
THE PRICE OF FREEDOM 43
VOICEMAIL 45
OPEN LETTER TO THE MAN WHO WANTED ONLY TO LOVE ME 47
PSA 51
PLUCKING CANTALOUPE 53
I'M SORRY 55
THANK YOU 59
JUST FRIENDS 61
THE RIVER SERIES 63
NOTEBOOKS 67
HOME 69
I KNOW PT 2 71

*To the many of you, with love,
light and anonymity. Thank you.*

I KNOW PT 1

I know God.
I know pain.
I know hearts can break.
I know broken hearts can break hearts.
I know one rotten piece of fruit can rot the whole bag.
I know God.
I know I come from a place that doesn't exist anymore.
I know evil.
    I've met him, showered in his mother's house and shared a bed with him. I kissed him and believed him when he called me beautiful.
I know God.
I know I am worthy, even when I don't believe in me.
I know I'm free, even when I feel chained.
I know God.
I know there is a purpose for me.
I know I'm loved, even when I don't want to be.
I know love and how it runs deep.
I know I want to cry, even though I don't know how to anymore.
I know I want to be held, even though I avoid vulnerability like a
    hole in my head.
I know I have a heart, even though I don't always feel it beating.
I know God.
I know Jeremiah 29:11
    —For God has plans for sinners like me.
I know these things weren't anyone's fault.

I know none of us are alone.
I know I've known rivers.
I know the miles are few, even though they've been long.
I know it's hard to breathe sometimes.
I know it's hard to believe I'm alive.
I know I shouldn't be here.
                        But...
I know a God with room in the kingdom for the conflicted like me.
I know through it all He will always love me.
I know He forgives me, even when I'm tired of saying sorry.
                        I know I don't know much...

BLACK WOMAN

I am a Black woman, born of Black women. The only
thing we lay with more intent and precision than
our dreams, are our edges. And they've already told
you the Blacker the berry, the sweeter the juice. But
I never knew that white people could be so thirsty or
that my blood could be so nutritious. And hear me say
this: after you breed your best for their best, you can't
be mad that this is what's next.

    Now I stand before you like whiskey in
    a champagne flute—the contingency plan to every
    other contingency plan. So, if you want to test
    this, I suggest
                                  you guess again.

CANVAS

if i told you i was everything you needed, would you
believe me?
i am the greatest beginning that i am afraid to start.
i am fresh
    and crisp
        and ready
                and waiting to be the kind of
                beautiful that you only see when
                you close your eyes.
strokes brush past me and paint all over my body,
leaving marks as deep as the eye can see.
            and I can see that you love me.
as long as i allow you to color me how you want me.
to leave the reds and browns and [B]lacks that you
want me to be.
the type of stained that you leave on walls hanging up.
        the type of altered clean that you
        claim as perfect.
            as long as the price is right
    as long as the end result is bright
      *as long as I forget myself to be what you
      believed I could.
when you see me in your sleep, shut my light to give
all of me away to give a way for you to be great, i must
first release everything I wanted.
but who told you i didn't have beauty in me?
    who told you i wasn't good enough to be
    by myself?

who told you your vision of me after you
was better than me before myself?
and after you finish, leaving me sticky and dripping
and tainted and unrecognizable to whoever met me,
including myself, you introduced me to the world as:
    your best
    your beautiful
             this masterpiece.
i wonder how long it would take to find a way back
to me. i wonder if i would ever go back to when i was
fresh and crisp and ready.
i wonder if i would've ever been the same kind
of beautiful from before you decided to paint me
gorgeous...
i wonder if when the lights go off
    and the cameras stop shuttering
        and the people stop staring
           and i get but moments by myself
                will i see any remnant of who
                i used to be?
will i believe in the dream i had for my masterpiece?
    will i see a vision of my Master in peace?
    will i be good enough to just be?
        will i remember when i was good enough
        to be me?
will i ever again be everything i could ever need?
            will i ever believe in me?

HUH
let me have myself?
beg for the wealth of social privilege?
black boys bring guns to the scrimmage?
lay bodies in the street because they challenge what you think?
spell beauty w-h-i-t-e but inspiration b-l-a-c-k?

BETTER DAYS

i was asked why the children stopped
believing in better days.
i'm not sure if our parents understand how they
paved this way. they set up a world where culture
plays hawk, and practice plays vulture, and to the
remnant of childhood—our minds are in torture.
cold?
                            they want you shivering.
tired?
                            they want you delirious.
hungry?
                            they want you starved.
trapped?
                            they want you behind bars
    lock away the mind and throw out
    our psyche.
can't you see, to 90's babies, we are the last of a
dying breed?
you tell us to believe but our examples are
endangered, on the way to extinct.
love burns hotter than 2,000 degrees.
    and as hard as we try, sallie mae holds our
    degrees
        and reminds me of the privilege within debt.
i pay for my future with my tears because i've given
you all my teeth, and still you ask me to smile after
another deferment?
        meanwhile, we are sitting debating diplomacy,
        with men who paid cash for private diplomas.

but see, little Black boys on the west side saw their
brother die yesterday. and in return for his body, they
asked the corpse why he resisted, as if existence was
available any other way.
    after, exhausted and emaciated, they demand
    answers on why ancestors failed to blaze a way...
        ...how quickly some forget how crack was
        the new cocaine and became how we
        survived another day.
lie again with this falsehood of equity.
you wrote of equality in cursive, but your pen
wouldn't be cut into three-fifths of an eagle feather.
        no wonder education failed to
        emphasize the importance of
        context when we read, or are we
        too consumed by technology?
    who will make the app for the right shade
    of humanity?
    who will be our super man?
who will let us save our day?
who will see that I am no damsel?
this dress is not indicative of demands,
    your assumptions created our distress.
        or did you miss this too when you said her
        visa was
            declined?
the mind doesn't pay enough to buy the way through.
    but i was asked why the children stopped
    believing in better days...
            ...end poem.

SPARROWS

i sing because i am happy.
i have found my free.
there are eyes saved for the sparrow.
                                                 but still
i know he watches me.
    There are sparrows in caged cells who know
    my name.
    These sparrows will become swallows and be set
    free. They will come to find me. And yet, I stand to
    sing because I am happy they found me, and not
    the reason behind the feelings I'd forgotten.
I was young and said what I meant. I always mean
when I say to sing. Death wanted to come for me,
wanted to darken the memory of the day I changed to
be.
                When I became free.
I can drive off to be free in the night as long as I
return the next day.
                                          So I sing.
Sparrows have an eye watching everywhere they go,
but the one who filled the hollow of their holsters, he
watches me.
He tells me his I am to be, and bound to him are
shackles of the remembered.
    I owe members my blood as an apology.
And now, no matter how many years time let go, it will
always know that home is a place we release to know.
                          (never again safe to go)

There are sparrows in caged cells, and I know my
name stories they stand to tell.
Judge and jury—executioner, my body they'd sell.
But
until the day somebody
catches this body
to bury behind the love
of lost bodies.
                                          I will sing.
because happy
                                      because free,
        because I know my body the Lord has forever
        to keep.
                    because I know, He watches me.

JESUS IS COMING

Jesus is coming, Jesusiscoming
2 for 15
Racks
Free bands
Fight the man
Plato has a cave
Plato can't see
Cartoons
Hop scotch
Gin and juice
Pac ain't dead
Don't do drugs dontdodrugs
Stay in school kids stayinschool
Stay
Stay
Stay
Stay...

Momma had plans for me.
       I mean, all moms have dreams for their
       babies, but
              Momma had plans for me.
Her baby was going to be somebody.
    I was top in my class, won the spelling bee every
    year from
        1st grade until 6th...blame Adam Foster.

I was the only person in my school who could
spell hieroglyphics—

H-I-E-R-O-G-L-Y-P-H-I-C-S
Hieroglyphics—enigmatic or
incomprehensible symbols or writing.
I always thought that definition was stupid. Just
because colonizers couldn't understand it, doesn't
make it not understandable. But then again,
colonizers gon' colonize... Christopher Columbians
and the rest of the pilgrims.

But Momma had plans for me, I was going to be a
doctor, or a lawyer, or a graduate professor. They were
going to call me Dr. Haile Winston Ibrahim-Shakur.
    I was going to cure the world.
    I was going to be someone's inspiration.
    I was going to do.
But after Momma got killed and I had to go live
with foster family of the month, no one seemed to
care enough to keep up with my constant curiosity
of furthermore.
    I used to read Socrates and Langston Hughes
and Nikki Giovanni and Aristotle and Friedrich
Nietzsche and biographies of all the greats:
        King Tut and Nefertiti
        King Sonni Ali
    I used to read of Kush
        Carthage
        Mali
        And Mansa Musa.
I loved listening to speeches by Farrakhan and
Malcolm X.

                I was going to go see him, but he
                was assassinated.
That was a month before Momma
          And about 2 years before the rest of
          my mind.
Why do they never see mental illness in Black boys?
            Why did no one see a diagnosis in me?
         Why do I have no memory of losing myself?
Why did you stop looking?
                Why is it that I scream for
                help but no one hears me?
Is it that schizoid is a type of orated hieroglyph?
        It is that I'm Black and so the abyss of the
        system doesn't quite catch me?
                Too redundant maybe?
          Black boy and abyss feels
          too synonymous...
So I stand on corners
        outside of liquor stores
        across from churches
        down the street from shelters and
        crack-houses
        at the intersection of numb the pain and too
        hard to breathe.
I watch these new kids and wonder why they gotta' be
so hard.
                (as if this world isn't already
                damned to beat)
I stand here, a man
                trapped

In an abyss that stares back at a caricature of Mr. Jim Crow himself, with the fake black painted on his face, and I scream for help but all you hear is...

Free bands
Stay in school kids stayinschool
Stay
Stay
2 for 15
Diesel
Diesel
Sour Diesel
Don't do drugs dontdodrugs
Don't
Fuck Donald Trump fuckdonaldtrump
Free Assata
I am a God iamagod
Made of God
Royalty
Made Royalty
Alhamdulillah
Ah Eloheim
Ah Eloheim
Jesus is coming
      Jesusiscoming/jesusiscoming
      jesusiscoming/jesusiscoming
JESUS!
      come for me...

PURPLE-BAG SKITTLES

you invited me to venture in pursuit of snacks
(what was to be a defining practice)
i had no cash, so therefore, no snacks, but you shared
6 purple-bag Skittles,
now older, wiser and collected, we've discovered how
life isn't quite what we planned
but
through all the birthdays and tears and parties and
classes and packs of newports and candy
purple-bag Skittles will always be my favorite

CRAZY COASTER

When I was young, I found a thing I believed I wanted
in my system.
      a substance that changed the way I felt,
      thought and
           functioned.
                  But that was when I thought
                          lived
                          and acted
                          like a child.
Now that I am a woman I must live with my mistakes.
The crazy coaster—
      a path of twists and turns and flips/ not fit for
      a person of my caliber.
Don't get me wrong. I'm not cocky or boastful but
crazy
                          doesn't deserve me.
*I am beautiful and strong with a talent unable to be
held in bond.
    Yet every time I try to erase crazy out of my life,
    he calls me 2 days later
        wanting to take me out for the night.
I want to say no
      tell him that I have dreams and things and in
      my life he
           need not be.
But he just has to flip the script and make me smile,
so I actually want to stay for a while, and the next
thing I know, the crazy coaster commences again.
    And old feelings come back

    and old desires return
      and the same ol' same comes for me
          (again).
On our last night, you whispered my name
    calling me to you
    I couldn't run away.
My mind
  body
  and soul wanted me to flee from your grip on my life
  but you were holding onto me too tight.
My feet failed me so I couldn't escape...
     ...I knew I had to close the crazy gate.
And now it's time
Time for me to run
Run faster than I ever could
    run to a land that includes not the
    thought or miniscule mention of you.
I break the shackles that cling to my skin
    responsible for me to commit the sin.
I bow to no man
Thing
Or mind-altering substance.
      Baby, that means you.
I have a newfound love for myself that you could never fulfill. Sick from this
  I move on away from you.
*When you remember that you miss me, know you will get used to it.

NOT ANOTHER BROKEN-HEARTED BLACK WOMAN

To the boys of my past, dressed as men, telling me of the things that make me worthy,

                                        this is not for you.

I've written you narratives more times than Morgan Freeman could summarize. Spent more summers believing in stories than Vin Diesel could be fast or furious. I am no longer delirious. This series of experiences on repeat is more played than play-doh. I can't claim ignorance when I knew you were a no-go. You liked me because I was funny but baby, you look like Bozo if you thought I couldn't be beauty and beast. You thought I needed you to walk like I don't got my own feet.

    you assumed I loved you more than my own destiny.
    you told me you wanted the best for me then left me
            because I wanted to become the best of me.
    you tell the world I'd be best if I just left that piece
                                          of me.
                as if I'd never find peace in me.
    Too bad I wouldn't let you defeat the beast in me.

I will always be your favorite storm.

                                          but.
                                          this.
                                          world.
                                          will.
                                          never.

                              chase.
                              the.
                              thunder.
                              out.
                              of.
                              me.
I am the woman you could not stop. the woman who
wouldn't be bought. I see enough beauty in me, to be
bigger than the woman you don't even believe in.
You can't keep me nailed to no burning cross.
                    I handed you the lighter fluid.
Step out of my way before I Angela Davis you.
Harriet Tubman reincarnated to break Bresha out of
those chains.
Assata is waiting with Watermelandrea.
There is a revolution not even Oprah Winfrey
could televise.
          Your pussy hat lies didn't pay enough for me to
                         commodify my own culture.
Becky wants to be in the club, drunk as fuck, with
some shades on.
But if you catch me outside being ratchet, that's it.
Wannabe Black so bad?
          Catch a cop in your rear view...
                              how-bou'dah?
He pulls you over—gun already out the holster—
because to these vultures
                Black is synonymous with strapped.

I might be light-skinned/ have just enough melanin
some tell me I talk white/ but I still won't be right
enough for my story to matter.
We shout say her name.
                                         Scream for our slain.
              Set fire to our rain.
And yet, are forced to watch as they take
entertainment from our pain this cycle will continue
until someone sees that being Black is:
      more than new jays and a fat ass.
      more than rollin' a backwood blasting trap.
Being Black is:
1. having to be your own beautiful after they decide bantu knots not cool no more.
2. no one wants to drive the car with a hole in the floor.
3. no one speaks up for you because you are just another Black girl.

You thick
    but you not that lit
        so, you just another fat girl.
            And you got class in the morning so
            tonight
                you won't even be that girl.
But make no ill mistake...
            this is not another broken-hearted Black
            girl poem.
This is ode to the concrete that gave birth.
                                      (to pac's rose)

This is about the caged bird that had to die so that a blind woman could see reason to survive;
> so that Billie Jean's granddaughter Brenda would want to see who her daughter grew up to be.
>> So believe.

The Black girl is bigger than any empty promise of liberty.
> We stand tall and strong like statues.
>> Why else would they try to send us back so soon?

So to the Black girl who stares back at me, I love you; even though nobody wants me to.

STATUTE OF LIMITATIONS

I did a bad thing today and now I'm in trouble.
    I'm not sorry that I did it and no one can make me apologize.
But sister, I had to tell you because one day, you too, will do a bad thing.
It all started when I woke up today.
    I woke up an educated Black woman in America.
        I capitalized Black and almost lower-cased America.
    I cleaned my body, dressed myself and went to work.
                And I wasn't sorry for none of it.
    I walked around all day, switching my code and my hips.
                And at no point was I sorry.
Understand.
    One day, you too will wake up an educated Black woman in America.
        You will instinctively capitalize Black and almost lower-case America.
Someone will try to come and rid the world of you because of this.
    Be sorry for nothing.
        Because bad doesn't always mean wrong.
                And
            Black will always be good.

BLOODY SHIT

it was blood.
bloody boys, and their baby girls.
baby mommas with broken hearts.
and blue and whites bussin' nines through soldiers like frozen water pipes.
and these are all laid tonight.
but we the survivors gotta see it when we sleep.
with lead in our water, we throw up their blood when we eat.
this poison is killing us.
    why the fuck is Black so much more than skin deep?
us, the survivors, have been made in the image of God.
    She says address each of her children
    by name.
these broken Black bodies bend down onto bloody knees
brutalized because they be born Black.
they tell me tears are what happens after the mouth is silenced to speak.
but after the image of these beautiful broken bodies is burned into my soul, the broken begins to break me.
and I ain't ever been no expert but I'm hurt, and my eyes don't seem to cry no more.
but this smile behind lips that they pay for...this smile shall never default.
because after all
    I come from kings and queens.
and what mountain reduces itself to the plains?

ON THE GYNECOLOGIST OFFICE

it'll take me longer to write this poem than it took for that doctor to re-traumatize me.
i only came here to get back on birth control because God be damned if i want to be a parent and she tells me i have to get my cancer screening.
anxiety has already clipped my tongue and i can't remember any of the information they need.
all i can think is that the door is behind me,
           but my legs won't let me leave.
i look up with my eyes—burning from the tears i refuse to cry—
i am now half-begging for a hysterectomy. she asks if i considered the iud—10 years without having to worry about a baby. at this point, the fire in my left cornea is spreading to the right and i explain that I have been raped and...
it'll take me longer to write this poem than it took for that doctor to ask me who—
who raped me
my daddy? an uncle? i want to tell her
           somebody's daddy raped me, but it
           wasn't mine.
...but how do i explain that i don't know how many daddies have been here with me as she is, or how many of these daddies have daughters who will one day know the sting of duck lips or the freeze your knees do when your ankles slid into the stirrups and....

...it'll take me longer to write this poem than to explain that i don't want no inanimate object inside of me and...

...it'll take me longer to write this poem than it took her to tell me that i have to wait at least 3 years until i can guarantee that i won't become a mother to no Black baby they'd rather kill themselves, than let me save them the trouble and...

...it'll take me longer to write this poem than it took for me to fall so far from grace that i fight myself not to self-harm, to rip my skin like any of them ripped my clothes from my body, to scratch or scrape or find a new way to make bleed because God be damned if i can't make myself leave.

> knowing whether or not i have cancer is not worth it to me if it means i have to lay here, open and alone with a light shining on all of my traumas, crying silently as some doctor explores these parts of me.
>
> no.
>
> it isn't worth it if i can't go to work because i'm too exposed to the elements/ if i will find a new way to hurt myself even after i pleaded with my memory to just forget this 1 thing

it'll take me longer to write this poem than to reconsider suicide because you can't tell me my pain is not enough.

HALLELUJAH

i heard secret promises of better
    whispers of relief that would rain
        with a wrath stronger than any storm
    dreams of peace to surpass terrors in the night
when the day is done, sun gone to slumber, and the
music i am too tired to listen to, too scared to admit
sorrow, struggling to accept the simplest compassion
until
you sat next to me and said
                                  this too shall pass
and in that moment, all i had was all i had
    ugly
    &
    weak
all i had was all i had but it was mine and
through the lime-sour of my jaw,
i could only give but what i had
it was frigid-cold and unidentifiable—from the
broken, but it was mine and of the tears began the cry
                                      hallelujah.

COKE WHITE & RAPUNZEL

once upon a time, in a far-a-way place, i was
nothing but a little colored girl sharing my roof with
screwtape.
>found myself in a neverland i never thought
>i'd land in.
>>(they never talk about how peter pan
>>is about dead babies.)

i'd wake up every day and
>wash all the demons off my body and spit out my
>truth with the colgate, get dressed and with the
>last brush of blush
>>my war painted face was ready for the day.

All my niggas with me gang as fuck, if you want the smoke, we can make sumn bust
And it gets cold out here so I gotta keep some bloody shit around me because I'm anemic
known 1 or 2 crips because I'm dead inside like the aborted baby of a bulimic and
I might be light but my right will leave you left like the bus broke down

I promise
You ain't never knew a girl who gets down like me
because you never knew a girl who was down like me
pinned to the walls of an asylum
feeling insane
too afraid to look you in the eye because I knew
it was the portal to all the secrets and lies in my brain
(Psychoanalytic theory would have a field day
with me.)
No matter the attempts, I could never slay my subconscious.
But I knew if I died someone would say I asked for this
dying to hide from the death I'd done.

As if seeing the shit in my sleep was not enough/
I'm forced to watch the blood of my realities pour out of me every month.

Don't tell me you'll protect me if you'll leave me to wake up by myself in the morning
Don't tell me you'll protect me if you'll leave me by myself in the morning

Don't tell me you'll protect me if you'll leave me in the morning
Don't leave me in the mourning of a love that you never intended to carry through
    and don't judge me for how I carry things
    when we're through
        don't judge me as if I wasn't
        responsible for getting everyone else
        home—as if my hands have ever been
        big enough to box with God.

BEAUTIFUL TODAY

i want to be beautiful today, not for the
commodification of my
culture
i want beauty to match brains
    become the name my generation proclaims
    when they
        validate claims
    be who the world bows to.
    be the force that leads a horse to water and
    makes it drink.
be the motivation behind justification
        you call me beauty **because** you
        respect my beat
but i want to be beautiful today
    take back what you took with crack when you
    cut it from
        cocaine
    take back the definition when you put my
    ambition in your
        dictionary
    remind you why spice was scary
i be beautiful today

ICE WATER

You celebrate me for my renewal as if you weren't a
factor of my ruin;
    telling me praises and pride as if you never
    looked at me with fire after I burned you.
I burned in you   burned with you
    and together
We sunk deeper than the depths of our
collected depression.
Sunk as if falling in love was a reasonable option
knowing that
    black heart's love breed off the cold
    breathe in sleet from the mixing of rain
        and frozen wind and seep ice water
        through our veins.

Still, you say I am amazing.
        Call me majestic as if God
    wasn't notorious for using the sick,
    shut-in and murderous to prove
    himself before his murderers.
And his plan meant we had to be
    break each other's heart to build his
        intention's manifest.
So yes
    you love me.
You dream of me in the middle of the day
    pray for me when you fear weak
    lay with me and watch me sleep
you stay with me

    but could never humble off your feet,
      could never bow your body to meet me,
      could never see me how I see me.
*You don't see how bad I fight to hold onto me because you can't let go.
But have you ever held onto ice with your bare hands?
stared into the beauty of frozen water
and watch as the light of the ice crystals reflect the light around it?
No. You're too busy staring at me,
     at whatever beauty you believe me to be,
     watching as I reflect light, you don't even
     feel me freezing your fingers.
Your flesh begs you to let me go even though your mind can't get past me because I'm so shiny.
Before you know it, we are frozen.
    Should've never had our bodies in contact.
     Now you're frozen in my time.
      And I'm less bright.
The shadow of your hand blocking out my light.
      I can't shine with you here.
And despite your love for me, I melted to become new.
  Everything must find change or else it'll be stuck
       stagnant
       and lame.
So yes, you love me.
You pray for me.
You see me in your dreams and in the middle of your day.

But how much can you love me if you're begging me
to stay
                and take delight in watching as I melt,
                          to then find fury when I grow
                          flowers?

THE PRICE OF FREEDOM

I miss you on Saturday mornings when the sun peeks through my blinds.
I used to wake up to the smell of blueberry pancakes and the sound of Bill Withers singing about lovely days.
I miss you when I go to my Mommy's house and she asks me about my life.
I miss you when I dance,
    when I introduce myself to new people
        when someone asks me where I'm from
            when I ask them if they mean originally or most recently
                when I respond to either specification
        when I realize that I don't know anymore
    when I'm going to sleep, and I remember home only in concept.
You used to be so happy; to smile like life was amazing and laugh like freedom was actually free.
                          You used to remember me.
I'm not sure who was the first person who told you that you were ugly, but I remember when you accepted it.
I never knew who taught you how to hate yourself, but I love you.
                                It hurts—
                              loving you.
I don't know why I still do, but I love you, even though I don't know what you look like anymore.

I think I see you when I first wake up, running around
getting ready for work.
                        I want to tell you that I love my job.
                                      I do it for you.
I wake up **extra** early.
I **make sure** I look crisp.
I get to work before most of the others.
        I want to be ready when I see you
              when you see me
           when I see you see me seeing us.
I see us in my kids.
I love my youth, even though I don't get paid
enough to.
                        It was never about money for you.
I think that's why I do it.
I'm looking for you — even though I know you'll never
come home to me.
I walk in and out of work everyday chasing shadows of
a memory that I'm not sure belongs to me.
                      At this point, it feels like that's all
                      it'll ever be.
Memories are as much about what made them as it is
remembering.
            That explains why I cry so much now.
I remember
and I miss
and I love
                              and I release.
I can't wait until I stop looking for you.

VOICEMAIL

you always come home to me.
you know you love coming home to me.
        it's like you know you'll always have a
        home in me.
you come lay in my bed and we hold each other.
in every tangled
weaving
clutching, glimpse of ecstasy
        you release yourself onto me.
breathing out everything that hurts.
and breathing in everything that fills the place where
the trauma lives.
        i bet you can't breathe without me.
constricting airways conflicting your life source, you
need me.
        (that's why when it hurts, you seek me).
right never felt as good as when i make you feel wrong
enough to write out your life.

                white

                out

                your

                life.
        come, fall into my bed tonight.
lie with me.
        i'll tell you i love you
        and that you're beautiful
        and that i'll always be here.
                and you'll tell me
        everything is ok.

i raise my hands to you, making you hate yourself
until it feels better.
;;;;;;;;;;;;;;;;;;;;;;;;;;you know you hate it here.
;;;;;;;;;;;;;;;;;;;;;;;;;;;;;;;;happy?
;;;;;;;;;;;;;;;;;;;;;;;;;;;;this isn't you.
come, rest beneath me.
i'll tell you it's ok and you'll tell me you love me too.
i hit, we sip and drink nectar from the fruit that you
know has tried so many times to end you.
    you love it.
    you'll love this.
    come home.
    let it go.
        let me make you feel good (again).
        let me be the reason you feel good (again).
                      i miss killing you.

OPEN LETTER TO THE MAN WHO WANTED ONLY TO LOVE ME

Open letter to the man who wanted only to love me, I told you not to try 3 different times, but you thought it was a lie on the 4th until I broke your heart for a 5th. I warned you not to like me, and as I've told you, I mean what I say, and I said to run away.

I recognize you might not have heard me; you know, girls say things. It's all a part of the game. But I'm old and tired and I don't like to play. So, when I call, and you ask me to come over, keep this list of expectations:

1. If I don't show up drunk, it's because of the bottle in my purse.
2. I won't stay long—just enough for my voice to linger in your ear, a hushed whisper, a reminder of who whomever told you about.
3. I love movies, but we'll never watch one of my favorites.
4. You'll hear stories but never know the whole plot.
5. You'll kiss me, or at least try to, and I'll turn my face because I don't need you thinking about fate.
6. You'll hear about my friends, but you'll never meet them. And if you add them on Facebook, they may accept. But that's only because it's Facebook. And everyone looks like a star on camera.

And I hate silence so I'll say words to fill the space where you can insert feelings. But basically, if it doesn't involve the simple math, I don't want to talk about other subjects.

> If 1 man and 1 woman meet at 11pm, add a bed and subtract enough clothes, how long will it take before he wakes up and realizes she's gone?

...because baby, I don't sleep.
I'll be up before you and leave nothing behind. And I'll lock the door if I can from the inside.
> See I'm used to these kinds of locks...

> > from
> > the
> > inside

But back to this list, I guess that was number 10, so
> 11) I'll lie to you

> > I'll lie every time...

...make you think you know things just so you'll stop asking. And I'll read you one of my poems and let you think it's about you.
I'll let you think you're special because when I leave...
> > (Yes—I'll leave)
> ...It'll be easier for you to walk away.

It's easier to act in anger.
And if you see me outside, I'll play a stranger.
It's a gift.
> You're welcome.
> Say thank you.

And if you say it first, I'll eventually tell you I love you.
> But it's only because I like how that tastes on
> > my tongue.

Baby, I leave you with this:
You might get sprung, but remember that spring break when we talked until forever and you asked what I was holding back? I was sitting with you, thinking about food, because as I said in so many words, love is just not what I do.

PSA

Two things you can never do:
1} run from where you come from
2) use any and everything to fill the place where the trauma lives
It's not as easy as said but stop trying to fill the place where the trauma lives.

                                        Grow. Heal. Breathe. Live.

PLUCKING CANTALOUPE

You saw her. She was walking barefoot through the produce section of the grocery store.
She had on cut-off jean shorts and a t-shirt that said something about Morgan girls. She was plucking at the melons, trying to decide which cantaloupe was just right. Her grandmother taught her that...

> You later learn that her grandmother is the reason she doesn't trust love. But that's a story for another poem...

You saw her. She was racing down Market Street with a weekend bag over her shoulder and red headphones bouncing off her breasts. She was the most beautiful thing you ever saw.

> You later learn that beauty is her biggest struggle. But that's a story for another poem...

You saw her. She was sitting in a bar, dressed in black, taking shots of something dark. It was all she knew.

> You later learn that her great-grandfather looks kin to President Lincoln and assume (rightly so) that his favorite word was nigger. But that's a story for another poem...

You found her—waking in your bed, lacing up her runners on the way out the door. You had planned to make her breakfast with the melons that you picked after she taught you how. You text her later that day.
> She'll respond in about a week.

She's on her way back over. In about 15 minutes you'll hear trap blasting from her hatchback. You plan to

tell her that you love her today, but she leaves as soon
as the session is over.
She says she's late for class, but you don't believe her.
> You later learn that she doesn't want love
> from you. But like everything else, that's a
> story for another poem...

Put her back.
Leave her right where you found her.

> She left the cantaloupe that she didn't feel was ripe
> enough yet.
> She left the pen that fell out of her bag as she ran
> down the street to the train.
> She left cash at the bar before slipping away.
> She left you in your bed
> (again).

I'M SORRY

I never wanted love—couldn't let myself believe in marriage or a family.
          (I also didn't know how to love me.)
Ever since I was old enough to understand discernment, I knew my daddy didn't love me. My mom always said it wasn't his fault. He didn't grow up knowing how to love healthy. And our relationship was full of apologies—Daddy being sorry.
And so, my relationships with men started to sound a lot like
    "Baby, I'm sorry"
And I'd believe them, force myself to believe in them, fighting my friends sometimes because I wanted to be with them. I loved them, even when it felt like they would never feel the same.
          (I also didn't know how to love me.)
I'd take them on their apology and tell them I was sorry when I didn't have to be. I'd let this remnant of Jesus held up inside of me be the reminder of forgiveness in this shadow of sincerity. I thought I could love them out of hurting me.
          (I also never knew how to apologize to me.)
I read in the Bible how faith without works is dead, so I'd let transgressions fade away as I bathe in all this
    sorry.

I once met a man whose sorrys washed over me. Half baptized in the blood of my tears I was dipped in the water and came up sorry and few.

> (I also knew this wasn't love but I didn't want to love me)

One day I fell on my knees in the shower and prayed that God would make me free. And that was when all the years of apologies burned away from this indescribable pain inside of me.

> (I was tired of fighting to love when all of love sounded like "sorry.")

And now I understand that you love me and you're sorry.

> And you're sorry for hurting me but you love me.

And I'd let you be my world all wrapped up in "Sorry."

> And you tell me I'll always be your girl and you're sorry.

And that wasn't what you meant to be—you're sorry.

> (Except you weren't what God meant for me.)

And now here you are again. But
I love me.

> I'm sorry.

"Love is patient, love is kind. It does not envy, it does not boast, it is not proud. It does not dishonor others, it is not self-seeking, it is not easily angered, it keeps no record of wrongs. Love does not delight in evil but rejoices with the truth. It always protects, always trusts, always hopes, always perseveres."

1 Corinthians 13· 4-7 NIV

THANK YOU

To the man who decided my death was better than
breaking up with me,

I thought about you today. It was another Wednesday,
almost 3 years since the passing of where we began.
Me:
>> black in hand
>> tear in eye
>> anger in heart and emptiness
>> between my thighs
> And you:
>> a backpack full of contraband
>> a fully loaded 9
>> and the devil in your soul.

I could've had you touched, you know.
> could've called any of those who love me, you
> know.
> could've called the police on any of those
> nights almost 3
>> years ago.

But I decided on giving you opportunity, freeing
myself with the same that kept me enchained.
> You kept me in a type of underworld reserved
> for roaches and shadows of humanity.

But opportunity against the best of my
best judgement.
>> *God needed that experience
>> for me to fulfill some facet
>> of His glory that I have yet to see.

But I still remember that day. Your thumb and forefinger rubbed my semicolon chain as if it were a period.

> I prayed to the one who comforts me in the valley of the shadow of death
>> asked Him to soul-keep when my body makes its final rest.

And now, just about 3 years later, on the other side of a life I thought I'd never find joy in, I find myself thinking about you.

> Wanting to sit over coffee and chains and say to you,

Thank you.

If I never kissed you
and looked into your eyes
and hugged your mother
and drank whiskey on her couch
and smoked your brother's newports on her porch
and slept in your arms

I'd never learn how to find love in myself.
And I love that for myself.

JUST FRIENDS

I left his house that morning wearing the same thing I
had on when I arrived the night before.
And as I walked the blocks back to the bus stop, my
hips cried to me.
> Wanted to know why I only bring them
> around guys who don't care
>> about the rest of my body.
> As if these limbs and shoulders and soul were
> next to my body.

I didn't know how to explain that I detest my body.
I save thighs and breasts like the best of my body.
When they touch, I can detach what's left of my body;
leaving [myself] out_____
>> next to my body.
> *Turn hard to the left when he calls me and
> make sure nothing is left when I leave.

But I cried that night because again, I arrived
knowing I'd leave the next morning still wearing the
same thing I had on when I arrived. And...
>> ...after he explored those parts of me
>> (too drunk to leave) ...
> ...I knew he never wanted to be with me.

And I never cry, not like I dripped from my eyes that
night.
I waited for him to fall asleep because heavy and red,
like liquor-soaked berries, (again) my eyes sought to
pretend love in a man barely known.
>> Because I had no home,
> I took refuge beneath his baritone.

But he heard me cry and gently placed his hand on my shoulder.
Said it would be alright
                         said he meant
                         no harm
         (whatever was killing me in my sleep would
         not come near me in his sheets)
said to go back to sleep
and as he pulled me closer, reminded me that I was allowed the consideration of comfort.
He told me, before my leggings left my hips, that everyone was allowed comfort and even if we just cuddled, he was fine with me.
It wasn't until deep in his arms—not caring whose skin was mine or his, unconcerned with fears—my eyes in his. Believing, as if for the first time, a life that included more than my own 4 walls.
                        I saw that I had been hiding, drowning in the sorrows of my own vagina.
         These walls been knocked down more
         times than I cared to count.
This mistake...
         ...it was too late.
             But he saw me.
And I stopped believing in coincidence.
Our meeting had bigger meaning because God had a plan for me. And I finally was able to let that take over.
                   So yes, in short, I cried that day.
And I never felt better

THE RIVER SERIES

in a different world
at a different time
we'd be engaged right now, looking over destinations
for a honeymoon and naming our children.
and in this universe, we both have the careers we
want
the peace
joy
and families we felt were supposed to be.
we'd be simply, together.
and my ring would glisten with the type of elation
that fills a life.
you'd call me your wife.
i'd love you
my knight.
we'd drink lavender tea from a chalice/ watching the
sun rise over our bodies as we lay entwined
with one another.
we never knew we needed each other.
i guess really, we didn't/ but together/ we made life
(better).
i've changed since beginning my new life in jersey
but i'll always remember us.
our love lives in the shadows of 2006-c
next to the guts and ashes that scattered the floor
after we knocked over the ashtray.
i never meant to fall for you.
it was nowhere in our original agreement.
there was no room for sleepovers

>   or dinners
>   or movies
>   or trips to the store with your daughter
>> or sitting on the floor
>> of your apartment;
>> high as giraffe
>> nostrils, staring into
>> each other, with you
>> teaching me to play
>> chess again, or me
>> telling you about
>> my dreams, or you
>> giving me rights to
>> the remote and the
>> weed, or trips to dc
>>> or the river.

but that was where i fell in love with you.
my little black boy from east monument street,
skipping stones on a saturday in the summer.
> > **the river became our place.**

we left everything behind except the weed and the
malibu and
i followed you
> past discarded remnants of illegality
> and
> 4-wheeler tracks.
>> we never did go swimming, not that it
>> mattered.

we were already dipped in an us that only existed in
the shadows of our acceptance. just like the river

                tucked away behind no entrance signs.
that was why i cried on the last visit.
we only exist there
                                    at the river.

i knew this would be it.
it would be real this time.
but
i didn't think i wouldn't be ready.
...
i
got
my
things
and unfolded me from your car.
i leaned over and kissed you before watching you
drive away.
and in that moment
i knew i'd never see you
again.
*funny how i was always leaving town whenever i
found myself leaving you.

NOTEBOOKS

i want to learn to love you like a new notebook, with the clean sheets, lyrical streaks, twisting lines without worrying about being neat. as the ink of my pen creates new poems, i want our love to inspire new desires of what love forever could mean. the black of my bic stains, breeding new bars, and i want our love to be Blacker than the original panthers, with tenure at Tuskegee Institute. i want to learn love with you like my new notebook.

i want to fall in love with you like my first notebook. i learned words like i want to learn this configuration of 4 letters—2 vowels, 2 consonants but 1 syllable. i want to learn how to dissect you like i learned how to dissect a, b, c, d and e. i learned how to lay down and let the words pick me up. i want to lay myself down and have your love hold me up, trust-fall into your arms and know you will catch me. i trusted those pages to let my life fall between them, our Black love would show me how beautiful Black can be loved. really, i want to fall in love with you, like I fell in love with my first notebook.

i want to be in love with you like my last notebook. when this is almost done, i'll need one last place to leave myself. i want to leave that with you—the last words to tell my truth. when i'm gone, the remnants of seeds can lay to take root. i want to leave the last of my love with you.

over time, i've believed in lies disguised as you. but the love we'd know would ensue and forever be the

unfadable ink from the ends of my quill. my best
friend, at 99 I want to be in love with you still.
    my new,
        my first,
            my last
these notebooks know me better than dictionaries
    know definitions.
i want to love like your eyes realize my lies of being
fine and hold me until I mean it
        until i know i'm safe enough to tell
        you the truth.
but more than anything, i want to be in love with you...
                ...like my last notebook

HOME

and then i met a man whose body felt like home, felt like
i belonged next to it
        someone wanted me to come back
                like no matter how far i go i am
                always welcome here, safe here...
i met a man whose body let me rest next to it.
and he holds onto me while i sleep, keeping me together because he knows this world plans to rip me apart.
                plans to beat on my body
                until i am blacker than
                sycamore tree roots, use my
                blood as
                            fertilizer
and then pick off my children like unripe cherries—
not ready to be made into juice
        not wanted to grow into the fruit of our labor.
but this man nurtures my soul and fosters my spirit.
and for the first time, i come home before the end of the night.

I KNOW PT 2

I know when things hurt, I like to hurt myself.
I know I shouldn't mix tequila and moonshine, but I'll do it anyway.
I know I'm not a smoker but I'll still hit the jay.
I know I don't have 3 hands but I'll still triple-fist the aforementioned.
I know that closure feels good.
I know that I am not that same person anymore.
I know it feels good to feel good.
I know it can be nice to see myself through the looking glass.
I know it's ok to need help sometimes.
I know this life and experiences haven't been for me.
I know not to race the process.
I know any competition is a competition with myself.
I know there are so many things I want to do.
I know I am amazing.
I know I am strong.
I know peace.
I know I don't know much.

*But I know I know peace.

www.ingramcontent.com/pod-product-compliance
Lightning Source LLC
Chambersburg PA
CBHW020914080526
44589CB00011B/588